Carole S. Briggs

*Lerner Publications Company*
*Minneapolis*

1999

OCT

*For my mother, Shirley Roewert Augenstein*

A&E and **BIOGRAPHY** are trademarks of the A&E Television Networks, registered in the United States and other countries.

Some of the people profiled in this series have also been featured in A&E's acclaimed BIOGRAPHY series, which is available on videocassette from A&E Home Video. Call 1-800-423-1212 to order.

Revised edition published 1999
Copyright © 1999, 1988 by Lerner Publications Company

Lerner Publications Company
241 First Avenue North
Minneapolis, MN 55401

Website address: www.lernerbooks.com

Library of Congress Cataloging-in-Publication Data

Briggs, Carole S.
    Women in space / by Carole S. Briggs.
        p. cm. — (A & E biography)
    Includes bibliographical references and index.
    Summary: Profiles some of the women, including two Russians, who have had important roles in space exploration and provides a brief history of the U.S. space program.
    ISBN 0-8225-4937-9 (alk. paper)
    1. Women astronauts——United States—Juvenile literature.  2. Women astronauts—Soviet Union—Biography—Juvenile literature.
    3. Astronautics—United States—History—Juvenile literature.
    4. Astronautics—Soviet Union—History—Juvenile literature.
    [1. Women astronauts.  2. Astronauts.  3. Astronautics.  4. Women— Biography.]  I. Title.  II. Series.
    TL789.85.A1B75    1999
    629.45'0082—dc21
                                                                98-2916

Manufactured in the United States of America
1 2 3 4 5 6 – JR – 04 03 02 01 00 99

# CONTENTS

*U.S. astronaut Sally Ride made history as part of the seventh space shuttle mission. Other crew members were:* front center, *Robert Crippen;* front right, *Rick Hauck;* rear left, *John Fabian; and* rear right, *Norman Thagard.*

# INTRODUCTION

**T**HREE, TWO, ONE. LADIES AND GENTLEMEN, WE have liftoff and America's first woman astronaut!" On June 18, 1983, amid the roar of two giant booster rockets and three powerful engines, Sally K. Ride and her crewmates shot up and into outer space. Millions of women were at Cape Canaveral in body or in spirit, wishing her well, their hearts full of pride for what she represented. Women had climbed Mount Everest and dived two thousand feet into the ocean's depths. The time had come to reach the final frontier—outer space. Never before had NASA allowed a woman to travel aboard its spacecraft. With her historic flight, Sally Ride realized the dream of the women who had tried—and inspired dozens more to succeed.

## THE UNITED STATES ENTERS THE SPACE AGE

When Sally Ride soared into space, a lot had changed since the Space Act of 1958 created the National Aeronautics and Space Administration (NASA). Back then, only a small group of space projects existed: lunar probes, a communications satellite, rocket engine research, and a brand-new project, the first man-in-space effort: Project Mercury. Six months after NASA was formed, the first seven U.S. astronauts were chosen.

At first, NASA was strongly committed to building new facilities. It built a research center for space satellites: Goddard Space Flight Center in Greenbelt, Maryland. NASA also built two facilities to house thousands of engineers and other personnel needed to put humans into space: Cape Canaveral in Florida, and the Manned Spacecraft Center in Houston, Texas.

In 1961, Project Mercury showed that the United States could launch a person into space and bring him safely home. After a four-hour wait in a space capsule atop the Redstone rocket, astronaut Alan Shepard's space flight lasted a mere fifteen minutes. Television devoted a whole morning of coverage to describing the flight, the landing of the capsule at sea, the recovery of Shepard and the capsule, and Shepard's welcome back to Earth by President John F. Kennedy.

Less than a month before, however, the Soviet Union had stunned the world by sending a cosmonaut into space. Yuri Gagarin was the first person ever to orbit Earth. The United States and the Soviet Union quickly

*President John F. Kennedy presents astronaut Alan Shepard with NASA's distinguished service medal for becoming the first U.S. astronaut to reach outer space.*

became embroiled in a "space race" to determine which country had the superior technology and, ultimately, the better political system. Within weeks of Shepard's space flight, President Kennedy committed the United States to an ambitious goal of landing a man on the moon before the end of the 1960s.

On February 20, 1962, millions of people again sat entranced in front of television sets as John Glenn, Jr., made the first U.S. orbit of Earth. He orbited three times in *Friendship 7* during a five-hour flight. Everyone listened with awe as Glenn described the four sunsets during his orbits. Newscaster Walter Cronkite traced Glenn's path around the world, told viewers what the inside of a space capsule was like, and explained the dangers of the intense heat of re-entry.

A spacecraft goes outside Earth's atmosphere on any trip into space. When it returns to Earth, it has to re-enter the atmosphere like a high diver entering a pool. The capsule is moving at such a high speed that the air in front of it cannot move out of the way fast enough. Instead, the air stacks up and becomes very compressed, which in turn causes it to become extremely hot—hotter than the surface of the Sun. Each spacecraft has special features, such as a heat shield, that absorb or deflect the heat to keep the vehicle from burning up.

During the flight of *Friendship 7*, monitoring equipment indicated the capsule's heat shield was loose. If the heat shield came off during re-entry, the capsule would burn.

After the silence of re-entry when no radio contact was possible with the space capsule, Glenn finally radioed to Houston: "Boy, that was a real fireball." A huge parade was held in New York City to celebrate the hero's safe return.

In 1962, a year before the end of Project Mercury, Project Gemini was begun. Nine more astronauts—all male—were selected. Gemini would provide these astronauts with the experience of living and maneu-vering in space. Gemini astronauts would learn to ren-dezvous with and dock, or join, with another space vehicle. They would practice extravehicular activity (EVA)—moving around outside the space vehicle. Gemini was also the United States' first experience with sending two people into space together. Most of all, Project Gemini prepared the United States to meet President Kennedy's challenge of landing a man on the moon by the end of the 1960s.

*All of NASA's early space flights were devoted to advancing the agency's ultimate mission: putting a man on the moon. NASA reached that goal in 1969. Here, on the moon in 1972, astronaut John Young salutes the U.S. flag.*

Project Apollo took up the challenge. On July 16, 1969, *Apollo 11* set off for the moon. Four days later, the world heard astronaut Neil Armstrong say, "Houston, Tranquility Base here. The *Eagle* has landed." And as he took his first steps on the lunar surface, Armstrong radioed home those famous words, "That's one small step for a man, one giant leap for mankind." Before the Apollo program ended in 1972, twelve men had walked on the moon, collecting rock samples and carrying out experiments.

NASA scientists had always expected to work with scientists from other countries. In the first international venture, the Apollo-Soyuz Test Project, a Soviet spacecraft docked with a U.S. spacecraft in 1975. Together, Soviet cosmonauts and U.S. astronauts conducted experiments in space science and life sciences.

## NASA Focuses on Reusable Spacecraft

The next generation of spacecraft was developed in 1972 and is still in use—the space shuttle. NASA wanted a spacecraft that was reusable and would allow scientists from many countries to accompany their own experiments into space. Earlier spacecraft had been designed to be used only once and to splash down into water at the end of a mission. The shuttle would take off like a rocket and land like an airplane, over and over. Not only would the shuttle save money because it could be reused, but since scientists would go along to conduct their own experiments, the pilots would not have to fly the craft and run the experiments as well. In this way, more experiments could be done at once.

On August 12, 1977, the shuttle prototype, *Enterprise*, began a series of gliderlike flights. Attached to the top of a modified Boeing 747, *Enterprise* was released from the jet at 22,800 feet. Astronauts Fred Haise and Charles Fullerton guided it through a couple of turns, then lined it up for a runway landing. After five minutes, twenty-two seconds of free flight, Haise and Fullerton landed the engineless craft without incident. In a series of tests, NASA determined which approach angles to the runway were best, how well the shuttle could stop after landing, and trained shuttle pilots in guiding and landing their new aircraft. NASA had planned to equip *Enterprise* with engines for further tests, but funding problems forced the agency to skip the step. *Enterprise* was eventually placed on exhibit at the Smithsonian Institution.

In 1978, a fully equipped and space-worthy shuttle orbiter, *Columbia,* was attached to rockets that would carry it into space. The shuttle's launching power comes from three rocket engines near its tail, which are fed from an external tank of liquid fuel, and two solid-fuel rocket boosters. The external fuel tank is divided into two chambers, one containing liquid oxygen and one filled with liquid hydrogen. The rocket boosters simply boost the shuttle's takeoff power. They hold a rubbery fuel that burns at 560°F. Several early unoccupied rockets exploded when the intense heat burned through a booster's outer casing. Once the boosters are ignited, they burn until all of the fuel is spent. Then they separate from the orbiter and glide under parachutes to the sea, where the boosters are recovered to be refueled for later flights.

NASA tested the shuttle's structural strength by subjecting it to vibrations that simulated liftoff. A space mission has the greatest potential for failure during launch. This is because of the tremendous force it takes to launch a vehicle into space. To lift a shuttle, the engines produce thrust, a pushing force. The force of thrust must be greater than the force of gravity in

*The space shuttle* Columbia *undergoes launchpad testing in 1981.*

order to push the shuttle away from Earth. Together, the shuttle's five engines produce seven million pounds of thrust. This force could shake the shuttle and its fuel tanks apart if they were not properly designed or built.

Finally, *Columbia* was declared ready for launching. The first shuttle flights would be called Space Transportation Systems (STS) flights. The first four flights, STS-1 through STS-4, were part of a program to test the shuttle and its astronauts. The rest of the shuttle missions would focus on tasks for government and private industry and on new devices placed on the shuttle.

## STAYING IN SPACE

Once astronauts were able to travel into space and remain there for as many as sixteen days at a time, people began to think about living there for months at a time. The Soviet Union launched the first space station, *Salyut 1* (salute), on April 19, 1971. It remained in orbit for six months. A series of six more *Salyut*s were launched in the following years, but none remained in orbit for more than five years.

Not to be outdone by the Soviet Union, the United States launched a space station called *Skylab* on May 14, 1973. The plan was to launch *Skylab* empty, and then send up astronauts in an *Apollo* spacecraft to work in the lab. But launch vibrations tore away *Skylab*'s large sun shield, and NASA officials at first doubted whether the lab could be used. For ten hectic

*Despite damage to its exterior, Skylab stayed in orbit long enough for NASA to conduct the three missions planned with the* Apollo *generation of spacecraft.*

days, the crew of the *Apollo* spacecraft worked to produce a makeshift sun shield. Then they docked with *Skylab* to conduct their experiments. Three different crews inhabited the space station for a total of six months during 1973 and 1974. They observed the solar system and conducted numerous experiments— including some that studied the effects of weightlessness on the human body. By the mid-1970s, NASA was winding down the *Apollo* projects and developing the shuttle. No further flights to *Skylab* were planned, although NASA officials hoped the space station would stay in orbit long enough for an early shuttle mission to attempt a salvage effort. Unfortunately, the battered *Skylab* fell to Earth in July 1979.

The longest operating space station was launched on February 20, 1986, by the Soviet Union. *Mir,* which means world or peace, was designed with living and working quarters larger than those on any other space station—with room for up to six people. Exercise equipment was installed to allow crew members to keep their muscles toned and strong despite being weightless.

Through the years, specialized research modules have been added to *Mir*. One module has been used as an astronomical observatory, while another has been used for medical research. Shuttles from Russia or the United States can dock with *Mir,* and so can unpiloted cargo vehicles that bring supplies to the space station.

*Mir's* unpressurized propulsion compartment contains two rocket engines to keep the space station at an altitude of 186 to 248 miles above Earth. Outside the propulsion unit is an antenna that allows satellite communication with people on Earth.

Several astronauts from the United States have lived and worked aboard *Mir* for up to six months at a time, including Shannon Lucid in 1996. The third Russian woman in space, Elena Kondakova, had lived there for six months in 1994. She returned to *Mir* in May 1997 aboard *Atlantis* for a nine-day stay, becoming the first Russian woman to fly aboard a U.S. spacecraft.

The first group of female astronauts was admitted to training in 1978. From left are Rhea Seddon, Anna Fisher, Judith Resnik, Shannon Lucid, Sally Ride, and Kathryn Sullivan.

# Chapter **ONE**

# GETTING INTO SPACE

**U**NTIL **1978,** ALL OF THE ASTRONAUTS CHOSEN BY NASA were male. With the shuttle program came the selection of NASA's first female astronauts. Women were finally admitted to the astronaut program for several reasons. A new law, a new space vehicle, and new attitudes all made a difference.

When NASA was formed in 1958, President Dwight D. Eisenhower—an army general himself—had ordered the agency to choose only military test pilots for the program. Military pilots, he reasoned, had several advantages for the astronaut program. Because they already were in the military, records of their training and experience were readily available. They already had passed security clearances and could be ordered to Washington whenever needed. Because women were not allowed in combat, there were no female military test pilots—and therefore, no female astronauts.

The military requirement was dropped for the second group of astronauts, chosen in 1962. Several women had applied to the program and were put through the same qualification tests as the men. NASA then ruled that admitting women to the space program would delay the United States' goal of putting a *man* on the moon before the end of the 1960s.

This angered several women who were well qualified to become astronauts. Pilot Jerrie Cobb was the first woman to pass the tests. Her ability to control a space capsule simulator under conditions of pitch (a forward or backward somersault), roll (a wing-over-wing flip), and yaw (side-to-side turning) was declared excellent. She was able to float in water in complete darkness hours longer than any of the men. Dr. W. Randolph Lovelace of NASA's Life Science Committee from Project Mercury suggested that she be accepted as an astronaut, if only so the effects of space flight on women could be studied.

Cobb assisted Lovelace in recommending more women for the astronaut program. In all, twelve of the thirty-nine female applicants passed the same tests given to the Mercury astronauts. Cobb then wrote a report for NASA recommending that women be accepted for training in the space program. But there was only silence from NASA. Finally, NASA officials announced that only men would be selected for Project Gemini because women did not have experience as jet test pilots.

Cobb and the other women argued their case before Congress, still hoping to gain admission to the program. They spoke to the Committee on Science and Astronautics, which then asked NASA to reconsider its stance on admitting women. But when the list of the nine Project Gemini astronauts was released, all named were males.

Finally, in 1972, Congress passed an amendment to the Civil Rights Act of 1964 stating that a federal agency cannot discriminate on the basis of sex, race, religion, or national origin. NASA is a federal agency, so it could no longer refuse to accept women.

## SHUTTLE FLIGHTS BRING MORE OPPORTUNITIES

First, the entry requirement was changed, and then NASA's program itself changed. Instead of one- or two-person missions, shuttle flights were planned to carry up to seven people. And the shuttle would go up more often than NASA's previous flights—perhaps as often as every two weeks. NASA might have 175 shuttle spaces to fill each year. Different types of specialists, as well as pilots, were needed in space. Leaving out highly qualified scientists who happened to be female did not make sense.

In 1977, NASA officials announced openings for new pilots and mission specialists. More than eight thousand

## JERRIE COBB, PIONEERING ASTRONAUT

Although she was never allowed to train for and participate in a space mission, Jerrie Cobb worked tirelessly in NASA's early years for women to be included in the U.S. space program. At age twenty-eight, she had been a commercial pilot for ten years when she met Dr. W. Randolph Lovelace at a conference in 1959. Lovelace invited Cobb to be the first test subject for research on women as astronauts. Cobb trained for the multitude of tests by running five miles a day and pedaling another twenty miles on her exercise bicycle. She ate protein-rich foods to build muscle.

For about a week in February 1960, Cobb underwent tests to evaluate her blood, lungs, heart, ears, nose, and throat. At the end of the week, Cobb learned she had passed the Mercury astronaut tests. Then she took more tests. For the multi-axis spin test, Cobb sat in a padded chair that could spin in three directions at the same time. The experience was like turning somersaults, doing cartwheels, and spinning around at the same time. The pilot could steady the chair with a hand control. Cobb's ability to control the "capsule" was pronounced excellent. In yet another test, Cobb was placed in an underground isolation water tank and told to stay there as long as she could. With only her head above water, Cobb floated in complete darkness for nine hours, forty minutes. The men's record was six hours, thirty minutes.

In August 1960, Lovelace announced Cobb was ready to fly in space. Reporters and photographers rushed to cover the story; everyone wanted to know about the "lady astronaut." Cobb hoped she and the twelve other women who qualified during the next year would be admitted into astronaut training. Instead, she was surprised to be offered only a consulting role for NASA. When NASA firmly declined to add female astronauts to the program, Cobb and the others took their case to Congress, addressing members of the Committee on Science and Astronautics in July 1962. Cobb told the committee that not only had the women proven themselves to be physically and mentally capable of being astronauts, they also weighed less than men, used less oxygen, and ate less food. Those would be clear advantages in a small space capsule, she noted. In turn, the committee urged NASA to allow women to participate in space exploration. To the great disappointment of Cobb, NASA stood by its earlier decision.

Geraldyn Cobb grew up in Oklahoma, where her father was a commercial pilot who gave Jerrie flying lessons when she was twelve. To pay for additional lessons she needed for a pilot's license, Jerrie did odd jobs. On her seventeenth birthday, she obtained her private pilot's license. A year later, she earned her commercial pilot's license.

After graduating from high school, Cobb played semiprofessional softball for three years to earn enough money for a war surplus airplane. One early job was to patrol oil pipelines in Oklahoma, flying low over them and checking for escaping fumes and oil leaks. In 1953, Cobb landed a position with Fleetway, an aircraft ferry service. For three years, she delivered military airplanes from the United States to Peru, France, India, and elsewhere. After leaving Fleetway, Cobb pursued speed and altitude records, then was hired as a test pilot for Aero Design and Engineering. She was employed there when Ralph Lovelace piqued her interest in space flight.

After her efforts to win a space flight had failed, Cobb was deeply saddened. She moved to Brazil in 1963 and began work as a missionary pilot—flying doctors, missionaries, and medical supplies into isolated jungle villages, then returning to the city with villagers who needed hospital care.

people applied, and two hundred men and women were invited to Johnson Space Center in Houston for physical examinations and interviews.

In January 1978, fifteen new pilots and twenty new mission specialists were selected for astronaut training. Of the mission specialists, six were women: Judith A. Resnik, Margaret Rhea Seddon, Anna L. Fisher, Shannon W. Lucid, Sally K. Ride, and Kathryn D. Sullivan. Two more female astronauts, Mary L. Cleave and Bonnie J. Dunbar, were added to the program in 1980 as mission specialists. All of these women flew in space before the shuttle program was interrupted by the tragic explosion of *Challenger* in January 1986 that killed the crew of seven, including Judith Resnik. All shuttle flights were suspended for two years.

In the late 1990s, over twenty women worked for NASA as shuttle pilots and mission specialists. Selection of new pilots and mission specialists is made on a continuing basis as needed. Each group since 1978 has included women. The class that joined in 1987 included Mae Jemison, the first black woman to become an astronaut. In 1991, Ellen Ochoa became the first Hispanic woman to be admitted to the program.

Women easily fit into the space program. They underwent the same training and testing as men. NASA needed to make only a few accommodations for women. It built a women's locker room for the gymnasium at Johnson Space Center and changed the shuttle seats so they can be adjusted for shorter legs. The selection of personal gear that the astronauts could take along on the shuttle was expanded to include tampons, skin moisturizers, and hair restraints. Because working in a space suit on an EVA is especially tiring for a person's hands and arms, areas where women are often weaker than men, some of the women have found that they need to work at improving their upper body strength.

The Soviets and the Americans both discovered a benefit to including women in their space programs. Georgi Beregovoi, the chief of the Cosmonaut Training Center, once said, "We have noticed that in training and study, the whole work atmosphere and the mood in a room of men and women are better than in men-only ones. Somehow, the women elevate relationships in a small team, and this helps to stimulate its capacity for work."

## GETTING INTO NASA'S SPACE PROGRAM

Applicants are accepted to NASA's astronaut program as astronaut candidates. They spend a year in training and must be able to prove competency both in classroom subjects and in the field before they are accepted as full-fledged astronauts who can begin advanced training for a mission.

When NASA prepares to add astronauts to its program, it advertises. After it sorts through the flood of applications, it invites the most promising candidates to Johnson Space Center for interviews and examinations. Doctors ask the candidates detailed questions about their medical histories. Technicians measure their pulse rates during exercise to determine how strenuous a certain exercise is for them. To test for blood pressure problems or an irregular heartbeat, candidates jog uphill on a treadmill while attached to an electrocardiogram (ECG) and a machine that measures how much oxygen the person uses.

In one test, interviewees are sealed into spheres that force them to remain curled up in complete darkness. NASA personnel give them no idea how long they will be in the spheres. If a shuttle were to become disabled while in space, its crew members would have to zip themselves inside balls only thirty inches in diameter. These balls would protect them as they awaited a rescue shuttle. When the rescue shuttle arrived, its crew would grab these balls by their handles and drop them into the rescue shuttle. The astronauts might be zipped into their "eggs" for several days before "hatching." For this reason, it is important that an astronaut does not fear being closed into a small, dark space.

NASA's selection committee looks for people with strong science backgrounds who have also done something extra. Because astronauts must perform a large variety of tasks, the ability to learn outside the original area of study is very important. So is the ability to set a goal and achieve it. Astronauts must also be able to work well with others in close quarters.

*Astronaut candidate Kathryn Hire uses parachute line to make a fishing net. Such activities are part of the survival training every astronaut must undergo to prepare for unexpected landings.*

## ASTRONAUTS-IN-TRAINING

Once an astronaut candidate is selected, she moves to the training facility in Texas, and the hard work begins. All new pilots and mission specialists train for one year before they are officially accepted as astronauts. An astronaut must not only be familiar with her area of responsibility, she must also know how everything on the shuttle works. There may come a time when another crew member becomes ill, and she would have to take on new duties very suddenly.

Astronaut candidates spend many hours learning all aspects of the shuttle flight program. They take classes in flight mechanics, meteorology, rocket propulsion, computer science, upper atmosphere physics, astronomy, astrophysics, and aerodynamics. Their instructors come from the Johnson Space Center and from universities all over the world. There are no grades. Astronaut candidates study hard simply because they want to learn all they can. Because there is so much training and expense involved, NASA asks all astronauts to sign a contract agreeing to work for the agency for seven years after the end of training.

Not only does the training period challenge the trainees' minds, but their physical strength is tested to the limit. For example, a new astronaut-in-training must learn to parachute from an airplane over both land and water, in case something happens to the shuttle. Trainees practice inflating and boarding life rafts and being lifted out of water by helicopter. On land, they may be required to spend three days surviving with only sleeping bags, pieces of parachute, and small survival kits containing dried food rations, a knife, and a fishhook.

Perhaps the most enjoyable aspect of physical training for many astronaut candidates is the experience of weightlessness. Some of the early astronauts and cosmonauts had difficulty adjusting to microgravity in space. To help ease this problem, NASA accustoms astronaut candidates to feeling weightless by sending them on special jet rides. The astronaut candidates ride a KC-135 jet as it makes a series of arcs through the sky. Each arc begins with a steep climb and ends with a rapid descent. At the very top of an arc, the passengers become weightless for thirty to sixty seconds—barely enough time for them to practice moving around. Since the swoops up and down in the KC-135 often produce motion sickness, some astronauts have nicknamed it the "vomit comet."

Weightlessness can also be simulated in water by scuba diving in a training tank. When the diver balances the forces against her so the pressure of the water and of gravity pushing her down equal the pressure of the air in her vest pulling her up, she reaches neutral buoyancy. That means that she will neither float nor sink. This feels somewhat like weightlessness. All astronauts receive basic scuba training so they can practice moving around in Johnson Space Center's neutral buoyancy tank. A mock-up of the shuttle's payload bay can be placed in the bottom of the tank. Astronauts can simulate a space walk and practice using tools in a weightless environment.

Both pilots and mission specialists are trained to fly a jet called a T-38. Regular flying time in the T-38 allows pilots to maintain their flying skills, and it allows mission specialists to become familiar with these high-performance aircraft. In addition, pilot astronauts fly a Grumman Gulfstream II that has been modified to simulate the landing characteristics of the orbiter.

All astronauts are expected to keep physically fit. Many jog, several play racquetball, and all are encouraged to lift weights. Astronauts must be in good physical condition because muscles lose their tone in space, where they have no gravity to work against. The heart, the most important muscle, can lose its tone just like any other. In space, astronauts exercise on treadmills and stationary bicycles to keep their hearts strong, and they do stretching exercises for their other muscles.

After they finish their initial training, astronauts move on to more advanced training. They take courses in navigation and control systems and in payload deployment and retrieval systems. Instructors set up staged malfunctions and the astronaut is challenged to solve them. Astronauts also learn specific skills they need to survive in space.

Astronauts also spend many hours in the mission simulator. A mission simulator is a computer-driven model of the shuttle, complete with hundreds of switches, gauges, warning lights, and a window view. The astronaut "flies" this simulated shuttle under many different conditions. She learns what to do in emergency situations and practices docking with a space station and making a rendezvous with a satellite.

Once an astronaut is assigned to a mission, she works with the other members of her mission crew, rehearsing and preparing for the specific tasks the crew will be assigned. At any one time, there are nine such teams rehearsing at Johnson Space Center.

## FLIGHT CREW

Both men and women have flown as pilots, mission specialists, and payload specialists. Shuttle flights have two pilots. One pilot, the commander, may control the shuttle during launch and re-entry. The commander is also responsible for the overall success and safety of the flight. The other pilot controls and operates the

## PILOT QUALIFICATIONS

o qualify for a position piloting NASA's space shuttles, an astronaut must:
- be a U.S. citizen;
- have a bachelor's degree in engineering, physical science, life science, or mathematics (but an advanced degree is preferred);
- have at least one thousand hours of experience flying high-performance jet aircraft (test pilot experience is preferred, but not required);
- maintain flying proficiency by flying fifteen hours per month in NASA's T-38 jets;
- pass a tough physical examination;
- be between five feet, four inches and six feet, four inches tall;
- have uncorrected eyesight of 20/50 or better (correctable to 20/20); and
- have blood pressure no greater than 140/90 while sitting.

shuttle during the mission. Both pilots assist with satellite deployment and retrieval using the remote manipulator system (RMS)—a robotic arm. In 1997, two women—Eileen Collins and Susan Still—were shuttle pilots. Collins was promoted to commander in 1998.

Each flight also has several mission specialists. These crew members are responsible for planning in-flight activities. They plan for the mission's use of fuel, water, and food. The mission specialists must understand the experiments to be done, the equipment used on board, and the kind of data to be collected. They might see if bees can fly when weightless, or they might test human blood circulation in microgravity. They may also walk in space, use the shuttle's manipulator arm, and help launch and repair satellites.

The requirements for mission specialist are slightly different from those for pilot. Mission specialists can be five feet to six feet, four inches tall. Uncorrected eyesight must be 20/100 or better, correctable to 20/20. Most of the women who are now in the space shuttle program are mission specialists.

Often accompanying the commander, pilot, and mission specialists on shuttle flights is a payload specialist. A payload is the cargo a spacecraft carries, including scientific equipment used in experiments that take place during a mission. A payload specialist is usually a scientist who is familiar with the experimental equipment aboard the shuttle. Payload specialists are not hired by or trained by NASA as

*Astronauts from other nations have flown aboard NASA spacecraft in recent years as part of joint missions. Among them are:* left, *Roberta Bondar of Canada;* center, *Chiaki Mukai of Japan; and* right, *Julie Payette of Canada.*

astronauts. They are selected by the organization sponsoring the payload. The payload specialists do, however, train at Johnson Space Center so they will understand how the shuttle systems work, how to operate payload support equipment, crew operations, and emergency procedures. Payload specialists may include astronomers, technicians who repair satellites in orbit, or scientists from other countries who wish to carry out a particular experiment. Women from all over the world, including Canada's Roberta Bondar and Julie Payette and Japan's Chiaki Mukai, have flown on shuttle missions as payload specialists. Payload specialists spend from three months to two years working and training with NASA personnel before their flight.

*Soviet cosmonaut Valentina Tereshkova in the hatch of Vostok 6, 1963. Many years would pass before another woman flew into space.*

# Chapter TWO

# THE PIONEERS

**B**OTH MEN AND WOMEN FALL IN LOVE WITH FLYING, just as they do with sailing or skiing, or any other exciting activity. So it makes sense that as the Soviet Union and the United States began to explore space, first with unmanned rockets, then with satellites, and finally with humans, both men and women would be fascinated by the idea of space travel.

A woman, Valentina Tereshkova of the Soviet Union, made one of those early flights. Her love of space reached its peak in 1961, when Yuri Gagarin became the first human in space. Two years later, in 1963, Tereshkova realized her dream of soaring into space.

Nearly twenty years passed before women again received prominent roles in space exploration. By the

1980s, the U.S. space program had progressed beyond needing just a select group of pilots who could control spacecraft. The shuttle program had created far more opportunities, especially for scientists to study in space. Of the group of women admitted into astronaut training in 1978, astrophysicist Sally Ride was the first assigned to a space mission. In 1983, she became the first U.S. woman to travel in space.

The next landmark for women in space came more quickly. In 1984, Svetlana Savitskaya of the Soviet Union became the first woman to walk in space. Both Ride and Savitskaya downplayed the importance of gender in their accomplishments, but there can be no doubt they—along with Tereshkova—inspired other women to chase dreams beyond Earth.

## VALENTINA TERESHKOVA, FIRST WOMAN IN SPACE

In 1963, Soviet cosmonaut Valentina Tereshkova became the first woman to go into space. She had completed months of training that included parachuting onto land and into water, keeping physically fit, training in an isolation chamber, and being whirled around in a centrifuge—a machine that simulates the effects of high gravity such as that experienced during launch and reentry. She also trained as a pilot and practiced moving her body around in a weightless environment.

Tereshkova's space capsule, *Vostok 6*, was very similar to the *Mercury* space capsules used by the United States, except it had an extremely heavy outer shell. *Vostok* weighed nearly five times *Mercury*'s one-ton capsule.

Tereshkova, or Valya as her family calls her, had wanted to explore space for a long time. When Soviet cosmonaut Yuri Gagarin became the first human in space in 1961, Tereshkova said it was the most exciting day of her life. She loved the space program.

At the time of Gagarin's mission, Tereshkova was a cotton-spinning technologist at a cotton mill on the Upper Volga River in western Soviet Union. She had made several parachute jumps in her free time and dreamed of nothing but going into space. When she felt she had perfected her jumping technique, she wrote to Moscow asking permission to train for space flight. A few months later, she was asked to report to Star City, the cosmonaut training center outside Moscow. After working with her for several months, Gagarin said, "She was born for space."

On June 16, 1963, Tereshkova made world history. She blasted off in *Vostok 6* to become the world's first woman in space. Minutes after liftoff, she came within three miles of Valery Bykovsky, a cosmonaut who had been in orbit for two days in *Vostok 5*. As Tereshkova began her first orbit, she made radio contact with Bykovsky. "It's beautiful up here. . . . What gorgeous colors," she said.

"I am sitting beside you. We are traveling through space side by side," Bykovsky radioed back. Later that day, they sang a song together to relax each other for sleep.

*Tereshkova checks her gear after landing.*

The next morning, Bykovsky could not reach his space companion. His radio messages went unanswered. The Soviet Union's mission control also tried, but had no better luck. What could have happened to her? Finally, a sheepish voice came over the radio. Tereshkova had overslept.

On June 19, after three days in space, Tereshkova ejected herself from her capsule at a height of 4.2 miles and parachuted to Earth, landing near her capsule in a sparsely populated area of central Soviet Union. Dozens of local people flocked around her to ask questions and to offer milk, cheese, and bread in case she was hungry.

By design, Tereshkova's flight had taken place one week before a worldwide conference on women was to be held in Moscow. The women at the conference took full advantage of the opportunity to celebrate her accomplishment. England's Queen Elizabeth wired her congratulations to Tereshkova.

Six days later, Bykovsky and Tereshkova were welcomed at Moscow's airport by Soviet Premier Nikita Khrushchev. The two cosmonauts marched down a red carpet, he wearing his military uniform and she wearing a dark gray suit. Thousands of Soviets were there cheering.

The two cosmonauts and the premier led a limousine procession to Red Square. The second limousine in the procession held four of the cosmonauts who had already gone into space. In all, fourteen cosmonauts, four of them women, were present.

On November 3, 1963, Valentina Tereshkova married cosmonaut Andrian Nikolayev. Their daughter, Yelena, was born in 1964. Nikolayev and Tereshkova were the first pair of space travelers to have a baby after being exposed to the cosmic radiation of outer space. Apparently the radiation was not harmful, since Yelena was born without any health problems. After Yelena's birth, both Tereshkova and Nikolayev continued their cosmonaut training and their study of aircraft engineering.

Tereshkova never traveled in space again, but she won a seat on the Soviet Union's powerful Central Committee a few years after her flight. Her marriage to Nikolayev broke up in 1982; Yelena was their only child. In 1983, Tereshkova was honored on a new one-ruble coin. The engraving shows her in a space suit and helmet. She became a member of the Congress of People's Deputies in 1989.

## SALLY RIDE, FIRST U.S. WOMAN IN SPACE

With a payload of two communications satellites and seven "getaway specials," canisters containing various experiments, the space shuttle *Challenger* soared through the sky. On board was Sally Ride, one of the United States' first female astronauts. It was June 18, 1983. Ride commented, "You spend a year training just which dials to look at and when the time comes, all you want to do is look out the window. It's so beautiful."

Ride acted as flight engineer for this seventh shuttle flight, STS-7. She was responsible for ensuring that the shuttle's mechanical systems were performing properly. She had to understand each of the instruments on the flight deck and explain any indicated problems to commander Robert Crippen.

In addition, Ride and mission specialist John Fabian were to deploy, or place into position, two satellites. The *Anik C-2* communications satellite belonged to Canada. The *Palapa B-2* was a communications satellite belonging to a telecommunications company tying together Indonesia's three thousand islands. The satellites were carried in the shuttle's cargo bay, a large compartment that opens into space, at the rear of the shuttle.

Many of the astronauts' duties on shuttle missions are experiments or tasks—such as deploying satellites—which they do for paying customers of NASA. The income from these tasks helps pay the costs of training, equipment, fuel, and research for the space program.

Ride and Fabian conducted much of their work using the remote manipulator system (RMS), later named the Canadarm, which they and several Canadian engineers designed. The remote manipulator system is a robotic arm. It bends in the middle, like a human elbow, and rotates at the end, like a human wrist. Its "hand" is designed to grasp satellites. The Canadarm is attached to the cargo bay, outside the crew compartment, but the person operating it stays inside the compartment. The operator can see where the arm is and what it is doing via a television camera. The RMS can be used to pluck satellites out of storage in the cargo bay and prepare them for launching, to help build space structures, and to do many jobs outside the orbiter.

After seven orbits, Ride and Fabian prepared the *Anik C-2* satellite for deployment. They used the RMS to position the satellite for launch. *Challenger*'s on-board computer indicated the space shuttle was in the correct spot. The computer exploded the clamps that held the *Anik C-2* in the cargo bay and, using powerful springs, pushed the satellite out of the cargo bay and away from the orbiter. The satellite's own motor later adjusted its position and speed so it could assume a proper orbit. Ride and Fabian repeated this procedure to deploy the Indonesian satellite.

On June 22, Fabian used the RMS to lift the German *Shuttle Pallet Satellite* (SPAS) from the cargo bay into space. SPAS carried eight experiments, ranging from the measurement of solar-cell characteristics to the mixing of different alloys in microgravity. It floated as much as a half mile above *Challenger* for more than ten hours. Then Ride used the RMS to retrieve SPAS and the experiments. While Ride was retrieving SPAS, *Challenger*'s small control rockets were fired. This tested the effects of shuttle movement on the extended arm.

After six days in space, *Challenger* was to be the first shuttle to land where it took off, at Cape Canaveral in Florida. Doing this would save NASA the expensive, weeklong return trip the shuttle usually took from its normal landing site at Edwards Air Force Base in California, back to Florida to get ready for the next flight. Unfortunately, bad weather in Florida forced the shuttle to land at Edwards anyway. President Ronald Reagan jokingly chided Commander Crippen. "You didn't stop and pick me up off the South Lawn (of the White House) like I asked you to," he said.

Ride made a second shuttle flight on October 5, 1984. Her main task for this second mission was to use the RMS to deploy a satellite that could measure the Sun's effect on Earth's weather.

Both the most fun and the hardest part of being in space, Sally Ride would say, was the experience of

*Using a headset, Sally Ride communicates with Mission Control from the pilots' area aboard the orbiting* Challenger.

weightlessness. She enjoyed walking on walls and ceilings, but she was frustrated by the clumsiness being weightless brings on. "It will take you ten minutes just to open your clothes locker," she said. "You don't really bump into things, but you don't know how to control your body—so your legs go flailing in one direction and your arms in another."

Sally Ride had trained all her life to be able to control her body—and her mind—in space. She was born on May 26, 1951, in Los Angeles, California. Growing up, she thought she would become a professional athlete. She enjoyed playing softball and football—and then discovered tennis when she was ten. In her teens, she was a nationally ranked amateur tennis player. By her senior year at Westlake High, she was captain of the tennis team. When Ride was twenty-two and attending Stanford University, tennis pro Billie Jean King saw her play. King advised Ride to leave Stanford and become a professional tennis player, but Ride decided to continue her studies.

School was always easy for Ride, and she loved math and science. At Stanford, she chose to study for a doctorate in physics. Ride was a member of a research team that studied high-energy lasers.

A doctorate in any science takes a long time to earn. Five years is about average. The time is spent mostly in doing research on a very specific topic in the student's field. The student poses several detailed questions and then plans and conducts experiments to try to find the answers. Sometimes an experiment that a scientist has worked on for months gives unclear results or fails altogether, so the experiment has to be redesigned and begun again. The last year of work on a doctorate is usually spent writing a dissertation, a lengthy description of the research and what can be learned from it. Ride finished her doctoral work in 1978.

Ride also joined NASA in 1978. One of her assignments for NASA was as a capsule communicator (capcom) for STS-2 and STS-3. The capcom is an astronaut who talks to the shuttle crew from ground control while the shuttle is in space. The capcom relays messages from the technicians at Johnson Space Center to the shuttle. Often called "the voice of mission control," a capcom must understand everything that goes on during a flight. She must stay calm, and her instructions must be clear and precise because the life of the crew is at stake. The job of capcom rotates through the astronaut corps.

Once NASA announced that Sally Ride would become its first woman in space, Ride became a celebrity. She was interviewed for newspapers and magazines, television shows, and radio shows. She does not like being a celebrity just for being an astronaut who happens to be female. She considers herself a scientist, not a female scientist. She did admit to being flattered—but also embarrassed—when the people of Woodlands, Texas, voted to name their elementary school Sally K. Ride Elementary School.

Ride left NASA in 1987 to take a teaching position at Stanford University. A couple of years later, she accepted a position as physics professor at the University of California, San Diego, and director of the California Space Institute. She left behind a record of achievement and accomplishment at NASA. When she became an astronaut, Sally Ride became a role model for other women. Tamara Jernigan, who joined the space program in 1986, told one reporter, "Her (Ride's) acceptance as a mission specialist ... made me realize I had a chance at becoming an astronaut."

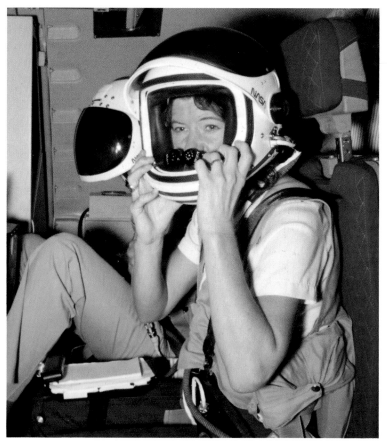

*Ride dons a safety helmet during a training simulation in preparation for her 1983 space mission.*

## SVETLANA SAVITSKAYA, FIRST WOMAN TO WALK IN SPACE

On July 17, 1984, the Soviet spacecraft *Soyuz T-12* blasted off from its launch site at Baikonar, bound for the space station *Salyut 7*. One cosmonaut aboard the flight was thirty-five-year-old Svetlana Savitskaya, making her second trip into space. Several days into the mission, on July 25, Savitskaya donned her space suit and followed Commander Vladimir Dzhanibekov out of the space station—becoming the first woman to conduct a space walk.

For more than three and a half hours, Savitskaya took turns testing a new hand-held tool—an electron beam gun that she used to cut through titanium, weld metals together, solder lead to tin, and spray coatings onto disks. The last task of her EVA was to collect samples left on the exterior of the space station.

An experienced pilot, Savitskaya had broken the women's speed record for powered flight in 1975, and in 1980, she had won the women's world aerobatic championship. Still, she must have known that her life would never be the same after flying into space.

Savitskaya had been exposed to aircraft since her birth on August 8, 1948. Her father, Yevgeni Savitsky, held the very high rank of marshal of aviation. He was a captain in the Soviet air force when World War II began. Captain Savitsky downed twenty-two German planes and was himself shot down three times. Once he even crawled from behind enemy lines with a fractured spinal column! By the end of the war, he had flown 360 missions.

Svetlana Savitskaya became a student at the Moscow Aviation Institute and, when she was fifteen, forged her birth certificate to indicate she was sixteen so she could make her first solo flight. Her father pretended to know nothing about the flight before it happened, but he could not resist coming to the airfield to watch her solo. He was proud of his daughter's well-executed takeoff, flight, and landing. When she climbed out of the plane, he greeted her with a chocolate bar, the traditional flyer's ration. It meant that she was officially a pilot. Also, by the time she was seventeen, Savitskaya had set three world records in parachute jumping.

Over the next ten years, Savitskaya graduated from the Moscow Aviation Institute as an instructor and test pilot, and she married a pilot. Savitskaya and her father both flew, often getting ready for flights together. When her father retired at age sixty-four, Svetlana was an expert test pilot and well qualified to become a cosmonaut. By the time she entered cosmonaut training at age thirty-two, Savitskaya could fly twenty different planes and had also trained as a mechanical engineer.

Savitskaya's training advanced rapidly, and the cosmonaut-researcher was quickly scheduled for her first flight, which would take place ten months ahead of Sally Ride's shuttle flight. Then, on August 19, 1982, Savitskaya, Alexander Serebrov, and Leonid Popov

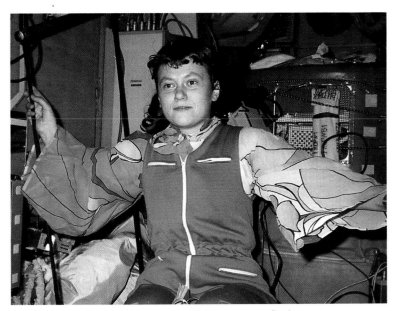

*Svetlana Savitskaya during her 1982 space flight.*

boarded *Soyuz T-7,* a capsule that was to be their home for eight days.

In space, Savitskaya carried out various experiments in astrophysics and metallurgy, as well as experiments on her body's reaction to weightlessness. During the eight-day flight, she also helped dock *Soyuz T-7* with *Salyut 7,* the space station that had been home to two other cosmonauts since May 1982. The crew left their *Soyuz T-7* capsule attached to *Salyut 7* and returned home on August 27, 1982, in the *Soyuz T-5* that had transported the resident cosmonauts to *Salyut 7.* The cosmonauts remaining in *Salyut 7* eventually used

*Soyuz T-7* to return home on December 7, after nearly eight months in space.

By the time she embarked on her second mission, in 1984, Savitskaya had been promoted to flight engineer. Along with crewmates Vladimir Dzhanibekov and Igor Volk, she visited *Salyut 7* again, this time in *Soyuz T-12*. The crew was welcomed with gifts of bread and salt, Russian symbols of hospitality, by the four cosmonauts who had been living in *Salyut 7* for several months.

Savitskaya proved very eager to start the space walk. Dzhanibekov moved out of the hatch first, bringing the new tool with him. He quickly found Savitskaya beside him. "Well, if you're so impatient, you'd better start," Flight Director Valeri Ryumin told Savitskaya from Earth. Savitskaya took the first turn, while Dzhanibekov recorded her actions on videotape. Then Dzhanibekov took his turn with the tool. On July 29, four days after the space walk, *Soyuz T-12* carried its crew safely back to Earth. Just two and a half months later, astronaut Kathryn Sullivan became the first woman from the United States to walk in space.

In the 1990s, Savitskaya remained on the cosmonaut reserve list, but the 1984 flight was her last. She had taken a position as a general aircraft designer with a Russian aerospace company.

Before her flight on *Soyuz T-12*, Savitskaya was asked how she felt about becoming the first woman to walk in space. She said, "A hundred years from now, no one will remember it, and if they do, it will sound strange that it was once questioned whether a woman should go into space."

*Savitskaya tries out a new piece of equipment during the first space walk by a woman.*

*With fellow astronaut Martin Fettman as a test subject, Rhea Seddon spins a rotating chair aboard* Columbia.

*Chapter* **THREE**

# EXPANDING WOMEN'S ROLES

**W**HEN ASTRONAUTS AND COSMONAUTS LIKE
Valentina Tereshkova were sent up in capsules during
the 1960s, the main purpose of the flights was to
prove humans could safely fly seven or more miles
above Earth. By the time Sally Ride flew aboard *Challenger* in 1983, space exploration had shifted to proving reusable shuttles were dependable for repeatedly
getting into space and back. Satellite deployment was
also a major purpose of the early shuttle flights.

However, once shuttle flights were able to consistently remain in space for a week, and satellite
deployment was almost routine, scientific experimentation became more important. The role of all astronauts, male and female, began to expand.

Since so many humans were now spending longer and longer amounts of time in space, scientists wondered how weightlessness and exposure to the Sun's radiation was affecting the astronauts. So NASA hired astronauts who were experts in human biology—physicians. NASA also began hiring chemists and geologists to explore how chemicals and different metals behave in a weightless environment. Shuttles became flying laboratories.

In 1995, the role of the astronaut expanded once again when a U.S. shuttle first docked with the Russian space station *Mir*. A year later, a female astronaut would live aboard *Mir* for six months. NASA began to study how long-term space exposure could affect humans.

## MARGARET RHEA SEDDON, CPR IN A WEIGHTLESS ENVIRONMENT

The crew of mission 51-D had a busy schedule. Because of mechanical problems on earlier flights, the crew's original payload was postponed for another flight. This crew had been assigned a new mission, and on April 12, 1985, the astronauts were finally aboard *Discovery*, awaiting liftoff.

The shuttle crew wasted no time beginning its projects. Less than ten hours after liftoff, the crew had successfully deployed an *Anik* satellite for Canada. Mission specialist Margaret Rhea (pronounced ray) Seddon had conducted some experiments to study how the heart pumps blood in microgravity.

The next major task was deploying an $85 million satellite, called *Leasat,* for the U.S. Navy. *Leasat* had been designed to be deployed without first being checked by the astronauts. This proved to be a disadvantage. Shortly after *Leasat* was put into orbit, Seddon realized its antenna had not come up. A lever was supposed to have popped into position to turn on *Leasat*'s electrical power when the satellite left the cargo bay. Apparently, this arming lever had jammed.

Back on Earth, NASA astronauts and engineers talked about different ways to solve the problem. Some astronauts went into a water tank with another *Leasat* and used various tools to see what might work to loosen the lever. Others climbed into the shuttle simulator to plan *Discovery*'s rendezvous with *Leasat* and to see how the RMS might be used in the repairs.

At the same time, astronauts and technical crew were debating whether *Discovery* should even try to repair the satellite. After all, no one knew exactly what the problem was, and the satellite did carry six tons of very flammable fuel. It could be dangerous for the astronauts to go near it again. The longer the satellite neither exploded nor turned itself on, however, the safer it seemed to be. Preparations went on for the repairs.

Finally, late on the third day, flight director Larry Bourgeois and his team designed devices that could be used to snare the lever. A team of astronauts led by Sally Ride built the snares from materials that would be on board *Discovery,* in order to make sure that the shuttle crew could build them. Then Ride's team practiced snaring the lever on the *Leasat* at Johnson Space Center. They worked around the clock to perfect a method, and then radioed instructions to *Discovery.* On the fifth day, April 16, shuttle astronauts David Griggs and Jeffrey Hoffman donned space suits for the first unplanned space walk of the U.S. space program. Within an hour they had the snare attached to the RMS. Seddon practiced moving the manipulator arm around the cargo bay with the snare on its end.

Very early on April 17, shuttle pilots Karol Bobko and Donald Williams used the rendezvous procedures that had been radioed to them. They brought *Discovery* within thirty-five feet of *Leasat.* Seddon began to move the snare into position. She succeeded in moving the stubborn lever three times. She even hit it once, just to make sure. It was all in vain, however; *Leasat's* electrical system still failed to function. Apparently, the arming lever was not the only problem with *Leasat.* Disappointed and tired, the crew abandoned their efforts and returned to Earth, landing at Kennedy Space Center on April 19.

As the space program began to mature, Seddon and the other astronauts got better at launching and retrieving satellites. NASA's focus began to shift to science experiments. As a physician, Seddon was interested in the life sciences—particularly how the human body responds to long periods of weightlessness.

Seddon's next flight was on STS-40, Spacelab Life Sciences. *Columbia* was launched from Kennedy Space Center on June 5, 1991. During this mission, Seddon and her teammates performed experiments that helped them understand how humans, animals, and cells respond to microgravity and re-adapt to Earth's gravity. They also tested hardware to be used on the planned international space station. *Columbia* and her crew landed at Edwards Air Force Base on June 14, 1991, after 146 orbits of Earth.

Seddon was also a crew member of STS-58, Spacelab Life Sciences-2. STS-58 was launched on October 18, 1993. In one of NASA's most successful missions, the crew aboard *Columbia* performed experiments on the effects of weightlessness on balance, the heart, and the lungs; the way cells use energy in space; and how muscles work in a weightless environment. They performed these experiments on themselves and on

*Seddon stands on a scale to be weighed before her 1993 mission aboard* Columbia. *The crew recorded all types of biomedical data on themselves before, during, and after the flight.*

forty-eight rats. *Columbia* landed at Edwards Air Force Base on November 1, 1993.

Margaret Rhea Seddon, who prefers to be called Rhea, was born on November 8, 1947, in Murfreesboro, Tennessee. She had wanted to be an astronaut since she was fourteen, when Alan Shepard became the first U.S. astronaut to travel into space. Although none of the astronauts in the program then were women, Seddon believed women would one day be admitted to the space program. She was determined to be ready.

She knew that any astronaut accepted for the program would need very special qualifications. Rhea decided that her special contribution would be to become a physician. In high school, she took math and science courses and worked hard at them.

Her parents supported her efforts. Her friends did not. They thought she would be so busy being a "brain" that she would never get married. Seddon, however, was undaunted. She enjoyed being a cheerleader, joined the Girl Scouts and Thespians, and became a member of the school newspaper staff, the science club, the Mathematics Honor Society, National Honor Society, and Latin Club.

Seddon graduated from high school in 1966 and enrolled as a pre-medical student at the University of California–Berkeley. Her first year there was a great shock. The university was large and very competitive. One-third of the class would not make it to the second year. Seddon knew her grades were not good enough to get her into medical school. Maybe, she thought, she should give up on becoming a doctor. She returned to Tennessee and enrolled in a nursing program at Vanderbilt University.

But her desire to be an astronaut would not leave her. After a year, Seddon returned to Berkeley, determined to study hard and get into medical school. She graduated with honors, receiving her undergraduate degree in physiology. She then went to medical school at the University of Tennessee in Memphis. During her internship and residency, she became interested in a medical specialty called surgical nutrition—the special feeding of patients who have had major surgery.

In 1975, between her internship and her residency, Seddon reasoned that a pilot's license would increase her chances of becoming an astronaut. Working nights in hospital emergency rooms, she took flying lessons during the day. Within several months, she had her pilot's license.

When NASA announced in 1977 that it would accept applications from both men and women for the shuttle program, Seddon was ready. She was thrilled when she was invited to Houston for a series of physical exams and interviews.

Seddon returned to Veterans Hospital in Memphis to finish her residency and await NASA's decision. On January 16, 1978, George Abbey, director of flight operations at Johnson Space Center, called to ask if

Seddon would like to become a trainee for the astronaut corps. Would she! Her delighted coworkers nicknamed her "Cosmic Rhea."

Astronaut candidate Seddon moved to Texas. She became one of more than 20,000 NASA employees at the Johnson Space Center. Like all astronaut trainees, Seddon learned to parachute through trees and power lines and into water. She lifted weights, ran, and took

*Seddon takes a meal break during her first space flight, aboard Discovery in 1985.*

classes in astronomy, shuttle design, geology, engineering, and computers. At the end of twelve months, she was an astronaut.

Because of her interest and expertise in nutrition, shuttle food became one of her specialties. People who would have to depend on shuttle food for long periods of time needed food packed with all the nutrients that would keep their bodies healthy. Seddon also helped design payload software, the computer programming needed for various experiments done aboard the space shuttle.

Her talents as a physician were also put to use in another way. She helped find a way to perform artificial respiration and cardiopulmonary resuscitation (CPR) on a person in space. During microgravity training in the KC-135 jet, she experimented with resuscitation techniques on a large doll. To Seddon's frustration, the doll kept floating away from her when she tried to push down on its chest or breathe into its lungs. Finally, Seddon and some of the other mission specialists devised a restraint that allows a rescuer to use her legs to push up against the victim.

On May 30, 1981, Rhea Seddon married Robert Lee (Hoot) Gibson, an astronaut and former navy pilot. They had met during their training and were the first U.S. astronauts to marry. In 1982, their son Paul was born. The couple also had two more children.

Says Seddon of her work with NASA, "I don't think a day goes by when I don't learn ten new things. That's my favorite part about being in the program. I'm probably going to remain an astronaut for a long time. I want NASA to get its money back for my training."

In September 1996, after 18 years in Houston, Seddon took a NASA assignment at Vanderbilt University Medical School in Nashville, Tennessee. There, her task was to help design experiments on the heart and lungs to be carried out aboard *Columbia* on the Neurolab Spacelab flight in 1998.

## MAE JEMISON, REDUCING SPACE SICKNESS

On September 12, 1992, women once again were celebrating a first. *Endeavour* (STS-47) was heading into space with mission specialist Mae Jemison, the first African-American woman to fly into outer space.

During the eight-day mission, Jemison experimented with biofeedback as a way to reduce space-motion sickness. Most astronauts experience nausea during their first few days in space. Floating upside down and sideways confuses the body's balance system, making an astronaut feel ill. Biofeedback involves deep relaxation to reduce the heart rate, slow down breathing, and reduce skin temperature. This seems to help control the symptoms of space sickness.

The *Endeavour* flight was also a Japanese Spacelab mission. Jemison and the other crew members, including Japanese astronaut Mamoru Mohri, used the pressurized lab to conduct experiments. One was an experiment to determine the effects of weightlessness on the fertilization and development of frog eggs. Scientists wondered if they would develop normally. When the shuttle returned to Earth on September 20, the embryos had turned to tadpoles, and on schedule, they became frogs.

In interviews given after the successful mission, Jemison told an *Ebony* reporter, "People don't see women, particularly black women, in science and technology. . . . My participation in the space shuttle mission helps to say that all peoples of the world have astronomers, physicists, and explorers."

Jemison was born October 17, 1956, in Decatur, Alabama, and moved with her family to Chicago when she was a toddler. She remembers wanting to be an astronaut early in life. As a teenager, she loved to read books on astronomy, and a favorite pastime was visiting Chicago's Museum of Science and Industry. Other interests included dance, art, anthropology, and archeology. As an adult, Jemison is an avid collector of African art.

Jemison graduated from Morgan Park High School in Chicago at age sixteen. She entered Stanford University on a National Achievement Scholarship. While in college, she played intramural football and produced, choreographed, and directed dance and theater productions. She was also the first female head of the Black Student Union.

Jemison has said she thinks it is very important to be well rounded. She is a good example of her belief.

Two months before the scheduled liftoff of Endeavor, Mae Jemison checks the panel in Spacelab-J that would be used to hold frog embryos.

Jemison graduated from Stanford in 1977 with degrees in chemical engineering and African-American studies. She then headed for Cornell University Medical College. During part of her medical school training, Jemison provided medical care to people in rural Kenya and to Cambodian refugees in Thailand.

After graduating from medical school, Jemison joined the Peace Corps as a medical officer. She was sent to Sierra Leone and Liberia in Africa to give medical care to Peace Corps volunteers and embassy personnel. She was only twenty-six. "I was one of the youngest doctors over there and I had to learn to deal with how people reacted to my age while asserting myself as a physician," she told a *Ms.* reporter.

In 1985, Jemison became a general practitioner in Los Angeles. The following year, she applied to the astronaut program. In February 1987, she received a call to come to Houston for an interview. She was accepted into the astronaut program that June. As is

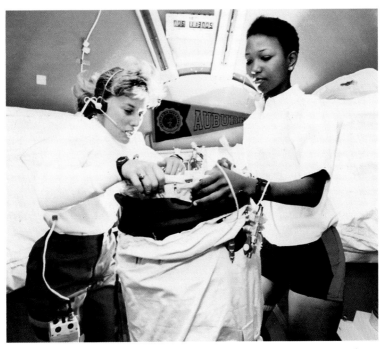

*Jemison and crewmate Jan Davis unpack equipment during the Endeavor flight.*

typical, she spent five years working for NASA before making a flight into space. After her successful STS-47 flight, she took a leave from NASA to teach a course on space technology at Dartmouth College in Hanover, New Hampshire. More women and minorities enrolled in her class than in any other undergraduate engineering course in Dartmouth's history.

Jemison felt her experience in the Peace Corps helped her to handle being one of only seventeen women and four African-Americans among the ninety-six astronauts in the U.S. space program in 1993. The other three African-American astronauts were male. While Jemison has been very much in favor of recruiting more African-Americans for the astronaut program, she does not like anyone to imply that blacks are just becoming involved in space. She firmly points out that ancient African empires such as Mali, Songhay, and Egypt had scientists and astronomers, just as white Europe did.

Mae Jemison resigned from the astronaut corps in 1993 to practice medicine. She also runs a company that develops and markets advanced technologies. Her company is developing a space-based telecommunication system to make health care delivery easier in developing countries. Jemison's credo is: "Don't be limited by others' limited imaginations."

She feels women should insist on being involved in the space program. Only by involvement can women have an equal say in the direction of future space exploration. Although she no longer works for NASA, Jemison would still welcome the chance to travel in space again. "I'd go to Mars at the drop of a hat," Jemison once told a reporter.

## BONNIE DUNBAR, U.S. SPACECRAFT DOCKS WITH MIR

The space shuttle *Atlantis* (STS-71) soared into orbit on June 27, 1995, at 3:32 P.M. EDT. The 100th U.S. launch carrying humans included mission specialists Bonnie Dunbar and Ellen Baker, headed with five other crew members for the Russian space station *Mir*. It would be the first time that a U.S. spacecraft had docked with *Mir*. Among the crew on *Atlantis* were two cosmonauts who would board *Mir* for a stay of several months. *Atlantis* would bring home astronaut Norman Thagard and cosmonauts Bladimir Deshurov and Gennadiy Strekalov.

Another goal of the mission was to perform joint Russian-U.S. life science experiments during the five-day docking with *Mir*. Astronauts also planned to do some filming with an IMAX camera, which would capture a very lifelike space scene. IMAX screens are curved and very tall, so moviegoers might imagine they were actually aboard a shuttle.

Prior to the rendezvous with *Mir*, Dunbar had trained for three months at the Gagarin Cosmonaut Training Center in Star City, Russia, to learn more about Russian space equipment. If a regular crew member had needed to return to Earth, Dunbar was specially certified to be able to take over that person's duties on *Mir*.

*Atlantis* also carried a Spacelab module so the crew could perform medical evaluations on the returning Russian cosmonauts. They evaluated the effect of weightlessness on the heart and lungs, the bones and muscles, and the immune system. With five original crew members and three returning *Mir* crew members, *Atlantis* landed at Kennedy Space Center on July 7.

*Bonnie Dunbar checks the fit of a cosmonaut space suit in 1994. She was the backup to astronaut Norman Thagard and was prepared to join the Mir crew if Thagard had been unable to make the trip.*

Having grown up on a farm in Washington, Bonnie Dunbar has felt close to the stars all her life. As a young girl in the late 1950s, she would gaze into the night sky, longing to explore that vast unknown. She wanted to be a jet pilot. Until the late 1950s, astronaut was an uncommon word.

Dunbar's parents, who had homesteaded their land in 1948 to start a farm, told her she could be anything she wanted. Dunbar's mother wanted her oldest child to be the first in the family to get a college degree.

The nearest town was several miles away, so Dunbar had few playmates aside from her family. She spent a lot of time reading. Her favorite books were the classics and science fiction. Dunbar's high school physics teacher encouraged her to use her strengths in math and science to major in engineering.

Since her first choice for a college was too expensive and her second choice did not accept female students in 1967, Dunbar opted for the University of Washington. She was excited about enrolling at the university as a ceramic engineering major because the program had been asked to develop a heat protection system for the space shuttle. This gave her the chance to participate in the earliest research on the tiles that would be used to protect the space shuttle during re-entry. She never told anyone that one day she hoped to be on the shuttle.

After graduation, Dunbar worked for Boeing Computer Services for two years, then began postgraduate work at the University of Illinois. Next, she took a job with Rockwell International to help set up production of the space shuttle tiles in California.

In 1977, Dunbar applied to NASA for the job of mission specialist, but she was not accepted. To broaden her background and increase her chances of being accepted the next time NASA took astronaut applications, Dunbar took a job with NASA which let her work with people instead of machines. Her job as a systems engineer was to take complicated engineering concepts, break them down into simpler ideas, and help communicate them to technicians.

Two years later, she reapplied to the astronaut program and was accepted. During her training at NASA, she also attended the University of Houston and earned a doctorate in biomedical engineering. Her specialty was studying how well human beings survive in space for extended time periods.

Dunbar's dream of jet flight also came true. Like the other astronaut trainees, she spent about fifteen hours per month rocketing at up to 800 miles per hour (mph) in NASA's T-38s.

Dunbar also spent many hours in the classroom learning star identification, geology, astrophysics, and more about the science of flight. She was co-anchor with Dan Rather during CBS's coverage of the second flight of *Columbia*.

Finally, after years of diligent preparation, Dunbar was scheduled to fly aboard the shuttle. The space shuttle *Challenger* soared into orbit on October 30, 1985. The mission had the largest crew ever: eight.

The astronauts split into two groups of four each. Working in twelve-hour shifts, they conducted forty experiments in the pressurized West German D-1 Spacelab. Dunbar was responsible for overall operation of the unit. She had trained for six months in Germany, France, Switzerland, and the Netherlands to learn how to run the variety of experiments supported by Spacelab. The astronauts tested the processing of certain materials, grew crystals, observed the behavior of liquids in weightlessness, tended a small garden, monitored the growth of South African frog larvae, and tested a device to precisely locate *Challenger's* position in space. Seven days after launching, *Challenger* landed at Edwards Air Force Base.

Slightly more than four years later, Bonnie Dunbar was on mission STS-32 aboard *Columbia* (January 9–20, 1990). During their trip, crew members used the RMS to deploy a satellite and retrieve the Long Duration Exposure Facility—a laboratory used in experiments studying the effects of long-term weightlessness and radiation exposure on the materials and systems used in spacecraft. In addition to experiments concerning crystal growth and the behavior of fluids in microgravity, the crew conducted experiments on inflight aerobic exercise and muscle performance.

Dunbar was the payload commander for STS-50, her third trip into space. She was responsible for the

*Dunbar talks to a group of middle school students.*

overall success of the shuttle experiments, of which there were more than ever. The shuttle was launched on June 25, 1992. It carried a space lab which would be used to conduct thirty experiments designed by over one hundred scientists working in teams. Four payload specialists were aboard to conduct the experiments. STS-50 landed at Kennedy Space Center on July 9, 1992.

Long ago Dunbar told a reporter, "What we need now is a space station. A space operations center would allow us to do some of the best Earth observations of weather, crops, and oceans, as well as service repair of vehicles." Dunbar's dream for space exploration has always been a space station, so it was fitting for her to be among the first astronauts to visit *Mir*.

Bonnie Dunbar is clearly excited about the future of space travel. She believes space programs will soon be involved in building space furnaces that can be used to make new kinds of alloys and crystals, and that outer space transportation is becoming commonplace. Sometimes science fiction doesn't stay in the realm of fiction—it becomes reality.

## SHANNON LUCID, LIVING ON *MIR* FOR 188 DAYS

The tiny speck became a bird-shaped shadow as it descended through the wispy clouds over southern Florida, quickly changing into something people on

*Shannon Lucid addresses the media on her return to Earth following a six-month stay on Mir.*

the ground could identify as the space shuttle. Gracefully, *Atlantis* landed on the tarmac at Cape Canaveral. The date was October 3, 1996.

Almost the second *Atlantis* stopped, three men raced aboard. The first man was a flight surgeon named Gaylen Johnson. He found Shannon Lucid, not lying on a recliner as he had expected, but standing near the exit, or hatch, of *Atlantis*. He quickly checked her pulse and respiration. Further tests over three years would tell scientists and doctors whether 188 days of weightlessness had changed her physically. The other two men used a pliers and screwdriver to help her take off her stuck helmet. Fifteen minutes later, Lucid climbed out of the hatch and walked twenty-five feet to the transporter that would take her back to NASA's operations building.

After living aboard Russia's *Mir* space station for more than six months, Shannon Lucid wasn't expected to be able to walk immediately on landing— when she would have to work against Earth's gravity again. However, Lucid had worked out daily with an exercise bike and a treadmill. This kept her heart muscle—and other muscles—strong. Ever the scientist, Lucid had wanted to prove that several months in space did not have to leave astronauts too weak to walk when they first got back. Astronauts and cosmonauts staying in space for extended periods before her had needed to be carried off their spacecraft when they returned home.

Lucid was the first woman to live in space for an extended time. Like men, women were moving into the role of space inhabitant. NASA needed to determine whether such long periods of weightlessness would be detrimental to an astronaut's later health.

Shannon Wells Lucid was born in Shanghai, China, in 1943, while her parents were in China as Baptist missionaries. The Wellses were taken prisoner by the Japanese during World War II, when Shannon was just six weeks old. When she was one year old, the family was allowed to return to the United States. After the war, Shannon and her parents went back to China, only to be expelled by the communist government in 1949. The Wellses returned again to the United States, settling first in Lubbock, Texas, and later moving to Bethany, Oklahoma.

Shannon graduated from Bethany High School and went to Wheaton College in Illinois. There she got a grounding in chemistry, but she was just barely able to pay her way. She worked in the student union and cleaned houses in order to earn money. When Wheaton raised its fees, Shannon transferred to the University of Oklahoma in Norman, where she earned a bachelor's degree in chemistry in 1963.

After college, she began working for the Oklahoma Medical Research Foundation and moved up to a research position as a chemist. She met her future husband, also a chemist, when he turned her down for a job. But Michael Lucid kept her in mind, and when a job opened up that he thought was right for her, he called to offer it. She took the job and eventually married Mike.

The couple had two daughters, and then Shannon decided to go back to school. She received her doctorate in biochemistry from the University of Oklahoma in 1973—and in the same year, she and Mike had a son.

As both a chemist and a science fiction buff, Lucid was fascinated with the idea of space exploration and life-forms in outer space. Before she married Mike, Shannon told him about her desire to become an astronaut, and they both agreed she should apply. In 1977, she learned NASA would accept female applicants for the first time. She applied and was accepted.

*Lucid straps on a football helmet for a water survival training session. In this exercise, she attached her parachute harness to a cable, then jumped from a high tower into water to simulate an emergency landing.*

Mike and their children have always been excited about Shannon's involvement in the space program.

The jump from researcher to astronaut may seem like a big one, but Shannon Lucid had loved flying since she was five years old. She holds a commercial pilot's license and has logged over fifteen hundred hours of flying time. One of her early career choices would have been to be an airline pilot, but the airlines were not hiring women as pilots in the early 1960s. Not surprisingly, Lucid's favorite part of astronaut training was flying in the T-38 trainer jet.

Lucid's first shuttle flight was in 1985 aboard *Discovery*. Mission 51-G had two goals. The first was to test the accuracy of a low-energy laser beam. Researchers at the U.S. Air Force Optical Station on Maui located *Discovery* with radar as it flew about 200 nautical miles (230 land miles) overhead. Then the laser beam was directed from Hawaii to *Discovery*. At its source, the laser beam had a diameter of one fourth of an inch. By the time it illuminated *Discovery*, the beam was thirty feet across.

The second goal of mission 51-G was to deploy *Spartan-1*, a free-flying platform that would allow astronomers to study the central core of the Milky Way galaxy. Lucid used the RMS to deploy *Spartan-1*. It flew free for forty-five hours, studying Milky Way's Perseus constellation, known for its distinct and beautiful stars. Lucid then retrieved the satellite for its return to Earth.

Lucid was also a mission specialist aboard STS-34 which was launched on November 22, 1989. On this trip, the *Galileo* probe to Jupiter was launched. Her third mission was aboard STS-43, launched August 2, 1991, to put a satellite into orbit. Slightly more than two years later, in October 1993, Lucid was again in space, this time aboard *Columbia* during STS-58. STS-58 was the first two-week shuttle mission. It carried Spacelab-J, a joint project between the United States and Japan. Spacelab-J is a pressurized laboratory that fits into the shuttle's cargo bay, giving astronauts more space to carry out experiments.

Lucid's stay aboard the Russian space station *Mir* may likely be her biggest legacy to the space program—and to women's involvement in the program. During her six-month stay aboard the station, Lucid conducted many science experiments and was herself an experiment. Over a period of three years after Lucid's return, scientists hoped to find out how much bone mass a fifty-three-year-old woman loses in a weightless environment. Just as important, scientists wanted to know how long it would take Lucid to regain any muscle capacity lost. They do not think bone mass, once lost, can be regained.

Psychologists wanted to study the psychological effects of a long stay in space. Lucid lived aboard a forty-foot space station with no one else from the United States for company. The cosmonauts covered the controls with red tape while they were off the space station, a clear message that she was a guest, not a crew member. For company, she had to rely on e-mail from her husband, and messages, books, and food that her grown children sent via a robot resupply craft.

*Mir,* however, is luxurious compared to the cramped space capsules the early astronauts endured. Residents can move between seven modules for a total of thirteen thousand cubic feet of usable space. There is a private cabin for each crew member. Up to six people can stay on *Mir* at a time, although usually there are only three.

Still, *Mir* is definitely not home, and during the last several weeks, Lucid reported counting the days until she could return home. Sponge baths, dehydrated food, weightlessness, and being without friends and family were among the difficulties of space travel she reported. She compared being on *Mir* to being stuck in a camper in the rain. Especially difficult was a delay in her return to Earth when a problem with the booster rockets—and then a hurricane—forced the shuttle that was supposed to pick her up to be about seven weeks late. She told reporters that she was looking forward to going home and inline skating with her adult children.

During her journey, Lucid orbited Earth 3,000 times and traveled about seventy-five million miles. No other U.S. astronaut—male or female—had traveled so far.

*The first female shuttle pilot, Eileen Collins, peers through a hatch.*

*Chapter* **FOUR**

# PILOTS
# AND SPACE
# EXPLORERS

**S**INCE **1977,** EVERY CLASS OF ASTRONAUT CANDI-
dates has included women. However, for thirteen
years, they were all mission specialists chosen to conduct science experiments in space. Finally, in 1990,
Eileen Collins was admitted into astronaut training as
a pilot. She was followed by Susan Still in 1994. By
1998, both women had turns piloting a shuttle into
space—and Collins had been named commander.

Female astronauts also continue to make important
contributions as mission specialists learning more
about outer space. They look deep into the universe to
learn more about distant planets and galaxies. They
visit *Mir* to learn more about living and working on a
free-floating space station. Most importantly, women

are involved in decisions as NASA ponders the future of its space exploration—helping to answer critical questions about strategies and processes.

## EILEEN COLLINS, SHUTTLE PILOT

The cockpit shook as *Discovery* began its ascent from the launchpad, with seven million pounds of thrust behind it. As the shuttle headed into the Florida night sky, a special group of women watched. Some cried. Calling themselves the Mercury 13, they were pilots too. In 1962, NASA had refused to accept them as astronaut candidates because they were not military test pilots. Instead, NASA appointed an all-male crew to join the Mercury 7 astronauts.

On February 3, 1995, these same women had a special invitation to see an important launch. Air Force Lt. Commander Eileen Collins had invited them. Some had flown bombers and trained World War II pilots. A few had flown fighter jets. They watched on this day as Collins became the first woman to fly a space shuttle.

Collins had not forgotten the women who flew before her. She carried a scarf that had belonged to Amelia Earhart. She also carried a certificate belonging to air racer Bobbi Trout. It had been issued by the Federation Aeronautique Internationale for setting a women's flight endurance record of seventeen hours, eleven minutes in 1929. It was signed by Orville Wright. The eighty-nine-year-old Trout, home-bound with a back injury, watched the launch on television.

*Collins and Russian cosmonaut Vladimir Titov sort through yards of pages sent from Mission Control to the orbiting* Discovery *during Collins's first space flight.*

STS-63 had an important mission, and Collins's abilities were critical to its success. During the launch, her primary responsibility was to monitor the main engines, the auxiliary power unit, the hydraulic system, and the electrical system. If anything went wrong, she needed to be able to correct it immediately. The lives of her crew members depended on her knowledge, cool head, and quick thinking. The shuttle's commander, James Weatherbee, turned control of the spacecraft over to her five minutes into the launch.

Four days into the mission, *Discovery* flew near *Mir.* NASA wanted to find out what kind of precision flying it took to approach *Mir* and dock with the space station, which it planned to do in the future.

Collins experimented with the exact amount of thrust to use and when to fire the engines so the orbiter could be maneuvered into docking position, although the *Discovery* crew did not actually dock on this mission. Collins also checked the normal systems during the flyaround to make certain they were functioning well. There was a problem.

A steering engine on the orbiter had developed a nitrogen leak. Collins worked with the team at Johnson Space Center to fix the problem. In turn, NASA's team on the ground had to reassure the Russians aboard *Mir* that *Discovery* would not hit and damage the space station.

On the fifth day of the mission, *Discovery* deployed a satellite. Weatherbee and Collins had to maneuver the orbiter away from the satellite. On the seventh day, they had to get the orbiter into a good position to retrieve the satellite. Once the satellite was aboard, two astronauts conducted a planned space walk. Collins took on the role of "space-walk supporter" as she coordinated the task. She talked to the spacewalking astronauts for nearly five hours by radio.

One purpose of the space walk was to test space suits. The suits would have to be redesigned to make them warm enough for the longer space walks required to assemble the planned international space station. The fingertips of mission specialist Michael

Foale's gloves reached a temperature below 40°F. Then he tried various assembly tasks to see how well he could do them. The gloves were so cold Foale could do little more than ball up his fists, which told NASA it needed to experiment with other kinds of gloves.

Three minutes before touchdown on February 11, 1995, the two distinct claps of a sonic boom were heard over central Florida. As with the launch, Collins's job was to monitor all systems aboard the spacecraft for the landing. *Discovery* touched down safely.

Eileen Marie Collins was born on November 19, 1956, in Elmira, New York. She was the second of four children. Her parents separated when Eileen was nine. The family lived in public housing and received food stamps.

Collins knew she wanted to be an astronaut in fifth grade, when her father took her to a local airfield to watch gliders. She graduated from Elmira Free Academy in 1974, and then put herself through Corning Community College by working full time in a catalog showroom. She received her associate degree in math and science in 1976. That same year, women were first accepted for military flight training.

This encouraged Collins to train as a pilot. She received her private pilot's license in 1977. She also attended school at Syracuse University and received a bachelor's degree in math and economics in 1978—the same year the first group of female astronauts began training.

Although the first women chosen for the astronaut program were scientists, Eileen Collins chose to become a pilot. She enlisted in the Air Force, where she took her pilot training and received a commercial rating. She became a T-38 instructor. A versatile pilot, she flew thirty different kinds of aircraft for the Air Force, logging four thousand hours in the air. She also taught mathematics at the U.S. Air Force Academy. She eventually attained the rank of lieutenant colonel.

In 1990, NASA accepted Collins for astronaut training. By 1991, she had finished her training, becoming the first female qualified to pilot the shuttle. Eventually Collins earned the last astronaut position never before held by a woman. In March 1998, NASA announced that Collins would be commander of *Columbia* during a mission slated for late 1998 or early 1999.

## SUSAN STILL, NAVY PILOT AND ASTRONAUT

The engines of the F-14 Tomcat screamed, and the air around the jet engines shimmered with the heat. The pilot, Susan Still, rolled it onto the runway and received radio clearance for takeoff. She kicked in the afterburner and streaked down the runway. The sleek gray jet shot up into the sky at a sixty degree angle and disappeared into the clouds. The jet was going more than 300 mph shortly after takeoff, but it was capable of a top speed of 1,544 mph, or 2.34 times the speed of sound.

Suddenly the noise from one engine began to fade in and out. Then it died. Efforts to restart the engine were futile. After practicing a few maneuvers with just one engine, Still headed back to the field for a landing. The jet's landing gear failed to move into the down position. The flaps also failed to come down to slow the jet for landing. A dial on the instrument panel was not working correctly, so Still could not get an accurate idea of where the aircraft was in relation to the ground. Meanwhile, the jet was rapidly approaching the field.

After discussion with the tower, Still decided to use a backup system which would get the landing gear

*Susan Still does a free float during STS-83 aboard Columbia.*

down. Finally, the flaps came down too. Even so, the jet was still coming in too fast. Personnel from the tower told Still they would do an arrested landing. She lowered the jet's tail hook. As the F-14 hit the runway, the hook caught on a wire stretched across the runway—an arresting wire. This stopped the aircraft and kept it from skidding into people or vehicles. To the amazement of other F-14 pilots who were watching, Still executed the landing perfectly and walked safely away from the aircraft. Susan Leigh Still had just become the first woman in Fighter Squadron 101 to pilot a Tomcat. It was 1993.

Born on October 24, 1961, in Augusta, Georgia, Still had never envisioned joining the military as a child. Since women in her family had traditionally been nurses, hairdressers, and secretaries, she had planned to become a hairdresser. One day, perhaps on a whim, she asked her father what he thought of her becoming a pilot. He encouraged her, and she later told one writer that she thinks her life would have been very different if he had not.

Still attended Walnut Hill High School in Natick, Massachusetts. During her senior year, she had to write a proposal for something career-enhancing that could be done in a month. She proposed to get her private pilot's license. Still soloed after only four hours of instruction and admits that she was quite scared. She kept flying until she had the forty hours needed for the license, thus reaching her goal.

Still graduated from high school in 1979. She received her bachelor of science degree in aeronautical engineering from Embry-Riddle University in Daytona Beach, Florida, in 1982. Then she moved north to take a job as a wind tunnel project officer for Lockheed Corporation in Marietta, Georgia. She completed her master's degree in aerospace engineering at Georgia Institute of Technology in 1985.

While at Lockheed, Still's boss arranged for her to speak with Dick Scobee, a veteran astronaut who later died in the *Challenger* accident. Still asked Scobee what she should do to increase her chances of being accepted into the astronaut program. He recommended that she join the military as a pilot. She took that advice and joined the Navy. Susan was a distinguished graduate of aviation officer candidate school and a distinguished graduate of the United States Naval Test Pilot School. She was named a naval aviator in 1987. After test pilot school, she reported to Virginia Beach, Virginia, for training in the F-14 Tomcat. She eventually attained the rank of lieutenant commander. She has flown over two thousand hours in more than thirty different aircraft. Still is an able athlete and musician who enjoys triathlons, martial arts, and playing the piano.

Still became the second woman to pilot the shuttle when *Columbia* was launched on April 4, 1997. The focus of the mission was experiments in combustion research and the behavior of fluids and metals in a weightless environment.

Two days after launch, astronauts discovered a problem with one of *Columbia*'s fuel cells. The cell was supposed to supply electricity for Spacelab and the orbiter. It had to be shut down and the orbiter crew began preparations for an early landing.

Commander Jim Halsell and pilot Susan Still began their own preparation for landing. They checked the surfaces of the orbiter that would be used to control the shuttle after re-entry. They also test fired the shuttle's maneuvering jets, which would be used to control the orbiter in space. STS-83 touched down at Kennedy Space Center on April 8, 1997.

## MARSHA IVINS, AEROSPACE ENGINEER

The three main engines were lit. The orbiter rumbled and began to shake. Seven seconds later, the two solid rocket motors lit and the shaking increased greatly as the shuttle lifted off the launchpad at Kennedy Space Center, heading for *Mir*, on January 12, 1997.

*Mission specialist Marsha Ivins*

This was mission specialist Marsha Ivins's fourth space flight and the fifth time an orbiter would dock with *Mir*. The crew's job was to pick up astronaut John Blaha, who had replaced Shannon Lucid at the end of September 1996, and to drop off astronaut Jerry Linenger, who would remain aboard *Mir* for four months. STS-81 also brought the Spacehab double module which would provide *Mir* with additional locker space for more experiments.

During the five days that *Atlantis* was docked with *Mir*, more than three tons of food, water, and experiments were moved onto *Mir*. *Mir* recycles two-thirds of its own water. To replenish the remaining one-third, U.S. astronauts took the water that the shuttle's fuel cells had produced and transported it to *Mir*. They passed ninety-five-pound bags of water from astronaut to astronaut in the style of a bucket brigade. Normally, the water would be dumped.

Ivins was in charge of getting the science experiments safely transferred. The Russians and the Americans jointly conducted microgravity and life science experiments while *Atlantis* was docked with *Mir*.

Born on April 15, 1951, in Baltimore, Maryland, Marsha Ivins wanted to be an astronaut from the time she watched Alan Shepard's flight on television in 1961. She began flying at age fifteen. Ivins's mother always became airsick and never liked flying. Ivins's father and grandmother, however, were flight enthusiasts who often rode along when she flew.

Ivins graduated from Nether Providence High School in Wallingford, Pennsylvania. When Ivins began attending college, astronauts were no longer required to be military test pilots. People with advanced degrees in medicine, engineering, or science were also needed. Ivins still had little hope of becoming an astronaut, however, since all of them still were men. Even if she could not be an astronaut, though, she reasoned she could at least work for NASA. After receiving her bachelor's degree in aerospace engineering from the University of Colorado in 1973, Ivins went to work for NASA as an engineer in July 1974. Part of her job was to work as a flight simulation engineer on the shuttle training craft.

When the space program began accepting women as astronaut candidates, Ivins applied three times. She finally was accepted in 1984 and finished her training in 1985, qualifying as a mission specialist. She holds a number of pilot's licenses and ratings, for everything from multiengine airline transports to gliders. She is a member of the Ninety-Nines (the international women pilot's association), the Soaring Society of America, the Experimental Aircraft Association, and the International Aerobatic Club.

Ivins's first mission was aboard *Columbia* in January 1990. Crew members successfully deployed a communications satellite and retrieved the Long Duration Exposure Facility (LDEF). Ivins's second mission was July 31 through August 8, 1992, aboard *Atlantis*. The crew members deployed a satellite and conducted a test flight of the first Tethered Satellite System (TSS).

Aboard *Columbia* once again in March 1994, Ivins and her crewmates took up payloads that studied the effects of microgravity on different metals and space flight technologies. They also studied how different space structures act when they are together.

Ivins loves chocolate. She invented a crumbless brownie that she and other astronauts could eat in space. In a weightless environment, crumbs floating around the cabin are a real nuisance. Ivins and the other "chocoholic" astronauts call her invention "nuclear brownies."

Being able to enjoy brownies aboard shuttle flights perfects the experience for Ivins. "Space seems to be equally joyful each time you go back. Anybody who's had a dream that they wanted to fly off a roof and keep going, there you are. When I got into orbit on this last flight, it was like being home. The vehicle tasted right, looked right, felt right," she told writer Carolyn Russo.

## TAMARA JERNIGAN, ASTRONOMER

Tammy Jernigan felt the familiar vibrations of the shuttle being thrust into space by what amounted to a controlled explosion. It was November 19, 1996, and she was aboard STS-80 for a very important mission. During the flight, mission specialist Jernigan and her crewmates deployed and retrieved the Wake Shield

*Tamara Jernigan, right, and Samuel Durrance look up information in a rotary file. The two were crewmates on a space flight in March 1995.*

Facility, a free-flying observatory that, in its wake, created a supervacuum one hundred times more powerful than any vacuum made on Earth. Using the wake shield's supervacuum, astronauts grew very thin film wafers to be used in high-tech electrical components. The wake shield flew directly behind the shuttle.

Fifty nautical miles later, the crew deployed Germany's *Shuttle Pallet Satellite* (SPAS). SPAS is made up of the Orbiting Retrievable Far Ultraviolet Spectrometer and the Extreme Ultraviolet Spectrometer. The instruments on board allowed scientists to study the origin and makeup of the stars. German scientists controlled the payload from Kennedy Space Center. The shuttle had to be flown carefully to maintain exact distances between itself and each of the spectrometers.

Jernigan had planned to take two space walks with fellow mission specialist Thomas Jones, but the EVAs were canceled because the outer hatch on the airlock jammed, and the crew could not get out of the shuttle during the mission. Jernigan and Jones had planned to test a crane that could maneuver large objects outside the space shuttle. They also were going to test a new tether for attaching an astronaut to an EVA work site. Both pieces of equipment would be crucial in building the planned space station, but they would have to be tested during a later mission. *Columbia* returned to Kennedy Space Center on December 7, 1996.

Tamara Jernigan was selected as an astronaut candidate in 1985. Born in Chattanooga, Tennessee, on May 7, 1959, she is a physicist, pilot, astrophysicist, athlete, and chef. She played varsity volleyball for Stanford University, where she received a bachelor's degree in physics and a master's degree in engineering. Then she worked as a research scientist at NASA's Ames Research Center in Mountain View, California, from 1981 to 1985. She returned to school at the University of California–Berkeley to work on a master's degree in astronomy, which she received in 1985. She completed her doctorate in space physics and astronomy at Rice University in Texas in 1988.

Jernigan has flown in space four times and acted as capcom in Mission Control for five space missions. Her first flight (STS-40, June 1991) was aboard the shuttle *Columbia*. Crew members performed experiments to learn more about how cells, animals, and humans respond to microgravity and then readjust to Earth's gravity.

The goal of Jernigan's second mission (STS-52, October 22 through November 1, 1992) was to deploy an Italian satellite called the *Laser Geodynamic Satellite* (LAGEOS). It was used to measure the movement of Earth's crust.

The crew also tested the new Space Vision System (SVS). Developed by the Canadian Space Agency, SVS is a computerized television camera and monitor system to be used for construction of the international space station. With the extreme darkness and brightness in space, astronauts have difficulty gauging precisely where an object is. SVS compensates for these difficulties. The astronauts used the remote manipulator arm to release a small target assembly. They then used SVS to visually track the assembly.

Jernigan's third mission was aboard *Endeavour* (STS-67, March 1995) as the payload commander. This was the second of the Astro observatory missions. The Astro observatory is made up of three special telescopes that use ultraviolet (UV) imaging to study the stars. Using data from Astro, astronomers hope to learn more about Markarian 66, a galaxy one-fifth the size of the Milky Way. Markarian 66 has stars up to one hundred times the size of the Sun being created at a very fast rate.

The crew took turns on a twenty-four-hour schedule, studying the far UV spectra of faint heavenly bodies and the polarization of UV light coming from hot stars and distant galaxies. Astronomers had observed one star's explosion just before *Endeavour*'s launch. They appreciated the unique chance to study such a phenomenon using UV observations. That had never been done before. They also took the first UV photographs of a volcano on Io, one of Jupiter's moons.

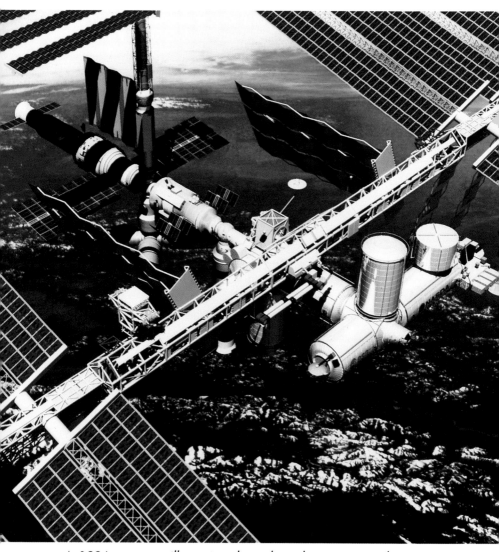

A 1996 computer illustration shows how the International Space Station may look when installation is complete.

*Chapter* **FIVE**

# BLAZING
# NEW TRAILS

**S**INCE THE EARLY **1980s, NASA** HAS BEEN focused on expanding the newest generation of space exploration—habitation. In cooperation with other space agencies, the United States is developing a space station where scientists will live and work for months at a time. There will be many experiments conducted in the various modules, but one of the most important will be the "human" experiment. All space agencies will study their astronauts during and after the long missions to find out how living in microgravity has affected their bodies.

Russia's space station *Mir* was launched in 1986. Like any aging machine, it developed problems. In February 1997, there was a fire on *Mir*, and its crew nearly had to evacuate. The next month, both main generators broke, and *Mir*'s crew had to use an unreliable backup system for oxygen. In April, temperatures aboard *Mir* reached the nineties, humidity soared, and antifreeze fumes escaped into the living area when the cooling system leaked. In June, a supply craft collided with *Mir*, putting a hole in one module and rendering it unusable. The computer system also failed several times that summer. A new, reliable, space station clearly had become needed.

Even when scientists establish an outpost in space, they won't consider their work done. Humans have never set foot on any planet aside from Earth. Doing so may be the next great challenge in space exploration. In July 1997, NASA landed a small rover, *Pathfinder*, on Mars. Before humans can even consider taking the forty-million-mile trip to Mars, they must gather information about the characteristics of the planet and its atmosphere. *Pathfinder* relayed information that indicates Mars is more like Earth than previously thought. Other probes have gone to Saturn and beyond as scientists look farther and farther from Earth in a quest for greater knowledge of the universe.

## THE INTERNATIONAL SPACE STATION

The United States, Canada, Russia, Japan, and the European Space Agency (combining resources from Germany, France, Italy, Belgium, Switzerland, Spain, Denmark, the Netherlands, and Norway) are working together to make a new space station operational—perhaps as early as 2000. Most of the countries involved have had difficulty funding their share of the station. No one wants to be left out, however, so everyone has scrambled for the needed funds.

Each space agency has responsibility for a different part of the station. The Russians will build the service module, a mechanism that will provide long-term position control for the international space station. The United States is building a module for a science lab. The Japanese are building a reusable platform that will hold different kinds of experiments. Canada is building a larger robotic arm.

Several female astronauts are helping NASA to make the international space station a reality. Ellen Ochoa has been directing crew involvement in the development and operation of the station. Nancy J. Currie was to be aboard the shuttle carrying the first hardware for assembly of the international space station. Susan J. Helms was among the first astronauts assigned to live on the space station, as part of the second crew scheduled for a six-month stay. Janet L. Kavandi is also assigned to the international space station project. Her job is to support payload integration for the new space station.

The astronaut class of 1996 contains several women from different backgrounds. No doubt many of them will also be assigned to important tasks on the international space station.

## SCHOOL-AGED ASTRONAUTS

T here is a place where school students can learn more about space and be an astronaut for a week. United States Space Camp in Huntsville, Alabama, is a summer camp for students in grade school through high school.

Operated by the Alabama Space and Rocket Center, space camp teaches its participants the science of rocketry and what it is like to work in the space program and fly on the shuttle. Sometimes actual astronauts mingle with the campers.

In just five days, campers build small rockets that really fly, build a structure while under water, work in Spacelab, and become part of a simulated shuttle mission. There are also United States Space Camps in Cape Canaveral, Florida, and Mountain View, California.

**In order to find out more about the space camps, contact:**

United States Space Camp
The Space and Rocket Center
One Tranquility Base
Huntsville AL 35805-3399
Telephone: 1-800-63-SPACE

## CONTINUING EXPLORATION OF MARS

NASA is planning to further explore Mars by launching an orbiter and a small lander in 2001. The lander will deliver a rover that will collect Martian rock and soil samples to be picked up by a future robotic mission. The lander will also hold instruments that will allow scientists to study whether rocket propellant can be made from gases in Mars's atmosphere.

The orbiter will be the first to use Mars's atmosphere to slow down and capture the spacecraft into orbit. How easily this is accomplished will provide important data for future missions. Using the orbiter, scientists will be able to conduct mineralogical mapping of the planet. They will also study the radiation levels in Mars's air and soil.

The robotic missions will gather information to help NASA decide if sending humans to Mars is feasible. NASA will have to answer certain questions before it can plan to send humans to explore Mars, such as: Will there be too much radiation in the air or soil for people to survive? Are there gases in Mars's atmosphere that can be used to make fuel for a return trip?

In the 1960s when President Kennedy talked about putting a man on the moon, he definitely meant a man. During the more enlightened age of the next century, the first human on Mars may very well be a woman. Perhaps the first broadcast from the red planet will say, "That's one small step for a woman, and a giant leap for the people of Earth."

# IN MEMORIAM

January 28, 1986, is a date that will never be forgotten by any astronaut. It was a very chilly morning for Florida. The nighttime temperature had fallen to 27°F and by sunrise was just above freezing. Mission 51-L had been delayed twice due to poor weather, but conditions finally looked favorable for a launch.

Friends and family cheered as the crew—commander Francis Scobee, pilot Michael Smith, mission specialists Judith Resnik, Ronald McNair, and Ellison Onizuka, and payload specialists Christa McAuliffe, a high school teacher, and Gregory Jarvis, a civilian engineer—stepped confidently into the launch area. Resnik, the flight engineer, took her seat on the upper deck with the pilot and commander. The other four crew members strapped themselves into seats on the mid-deck.

Like any explorers, the *Challenger* crew realized their mission was dangerous. They knew they were sitting on three enormous tanks of fuel that, once ignited, would continue to burn until all the fuel was spent. Even so, no one was prepared for what happened next.

Seventy-three seconds into the flight, an immense explosion stunned those watching from the launch-pad. The solid rocket boosters broke away from *Challenger*, still flaming as they fell into the sea. At the time, all the NASA commentator could say was,

"Flight controllers here looking very carefully at the situation. Obviously, a major malfunction." Little more than a minute after liftoff, the flight was over. All seven crew members were dead.

Ultimately, investigators decided a leaky seal caused the explosion. A seal between sections of the right booster leaked because it had gotten too cold (and had contracted) the night before and had not yet warmed up (and re-expanded) by the time of launch. This leaky seal allowed flames to shoot out the side of the booster. The flames burned through to the liquid fuel tank, which then exploded.

NASA recovered pieces of the shuttle and studied them, along with all of the data the shuttle's computers and sensors recorded during the flight. The booster rockets were redesigned and retested. The shuttle program was put on hold for two years until NASA was satisfied future flights would not be in danger of exploding.

In addition, NASA and a special commission of Congress examined NASA's decision to go ahead with the launch in spite of the cold. They asked who advised that the launch proceed and who made the decisions. In the end, some people at NASA were relieved of their duties, and some of the methods for deciding whether to launch were changed. The disaster was a costly lesson in human life, materials, and time.

With the *Challenger* accident, Judith Resnik became the first female astronaut to die aboard a space vehicle.

*The ill-fated* Challenger *crew:* Front row, left to right, **Mike Smith, Dick Scobee, and Ron McNair.** Back row, left to right, **Ellison Onizuka, Christa McAuliffe, Greg Jarvis, and Judy Resnik.**

Resnik had flown once before, aboard *Discovery* in August 1984. Another woman, Christa McAuliffe, the first teacher in space, was also killed in the *Challenger* accident.

Family and friends of the two women indicated that they would not have wanted space exploration to cease because of the tragedy. Resnik once said she had never been happier than she had been since becoming an astronaut. McAuliffe had looked forward to sharing her experience aboard the space shuttle with millions of students across the United States. She, too, thought the benefits of space travel outweighed the risks.

# GLOSSARY

**astronaut:** a person who travels into space

**capsule communicator (capcom):** the astronaut in Mission Control who communicates with astronauts aboard spacecraft

**cargo bay:** the section of the shuttle orbiter that opens into space and holds large equipment, such as satellites and extra experiment compartments

**commander:** the astronaut responsible for the success and safety of a space mission. The commander pilots the shuttle during launch and re-entry.

**cosmonaut:** a Russian astronaut

**deploy:** to place equipment, usually a satellite, into orbit. Aboard the space shuttle, this involves removing the equipment from the cargo bay and pushing it into space.

**dock:** to join one vehicle with another in space

**extravehicular activity (EVA):** astronaut excursions outside the orbiter in space; also called a space walk

**flight engineer:** the astronaut responsible for the mechanical performance of the spacecraft

**microgravity:** a term used to describe the condition of weightlessness in space

**Mission Control:** the ground-based unit of space workers who monitor and direct the activities of astronauts in space

**mission simulator:** a model of the orbiter's cockpit which stays on the ground but can be made to seem as though it is taking off or flying. Astronauts practice "flying" in it under different conditions.

**orbiter:** the portion of the shuttle that reaches orbit after the rocket boosters and fuel tank have broken away

**payload:** all of the cargo, including scientific equipment to be used for experiments, carried into space by a spacecraft

**payload commander:** the astronaut responsible for the overall success of the experiments on a shuttle mission

**payload specialist:** a person—not necessarily an astronaut—who joins a space mission to conduct specific experiments

**pilot:** the astronaut who flies the shuttle after launch and before re-entry and who backs up the commander

**re-entry:** the return to Earth's atmosphere after travel in space

**remote manipulator system or RMS:** a robotic arm in the orbiter's cargo bay and its controls inside the orbiter. It allows astronauts to manipulate items in the cargo bay without leaving the orbiter.

**solid rocket booster:** one of two rockets filled with solid fuel to provide extra power to the shuttle during launch

**space:** officially the area more than fifty miles above Earth's surface where there is no atmosphere

**thrust:** a forward or upward push created by gases escaping through the rear of the rocket engines

# SELECTED BIBLIOGRAPHY

Burns, K. and W. Miles, *Black Stars in Orbit.* Gulliver Books,
    Harcourt Brace & Co.: New York, New York, 1995.
Neal, V., C. S. Lewis, and F. W. Winter, *Spaceflight.* Macmillan:
    New York, New York, 1995.
Russo, Carolyn, *Women and Flight.* National Air and Space
    Museum in association with Bulfinch Press, Little Brown and
    Company: Boston, Massachusetts, 1997.
Weber, L., *Top Gun Fighters and America's Jet Power,* Publications
    International, Ltd.: Lincolnwood, Illinois, 1990.

**PERIODICALS**

Asker, J. R., "Shuttle/Mir Flights Pose New Challenges," *Aviation
    Week and Space Technology,* February 20, 1995.
———., "U.S., Russia Plot Shuttle/Mir Flights," *Aviation Week and
    Space Technology,* January 16, 1995.
"Astro 2 Reaps UV Data," *Aviation Week and Space Technology,*
    March 20, 1995.
Balter, M., "All Aboard the Space Station," *Science,* October 1995.
Covault, C., "Columbia Set for Dual Deployments, Retrievals,"
    *Aviation Week and Space Technology,* October 28, 1996.
Green, C., "To Boldly Go...," *Ms.,* July–August, 1992.
Gitelman, M. K., "Shuttle Pilot Eileen Collins," *Woman Pilot,*
    May–June, 1995.
McKenna, J. T., "Shuttle Payload Studied Volcano on Jovian
    Moon," *Aviation Week and Space Technology,* March 13, 1995.
Mecham, M., "Japan to Start Station Work With H-2 Launch of
    Platform," *Aviation Week and Space Technology,* March 13,
    1995.
"NASA Budget Request Keeps Station on Track," *Aviation Week
    and Space Technology,* February 17, 1997.
Sheridan, D., "An American First: Eileen Collins," *NEA Today,*
    September 15, 1995.
"Station Plan Expands Shuttle, Mir Roles," *Aviation Week and
    Space Technology,* January 29, 1996.
Trimble, J., "America's Magellan in Space," *U.S. News and World
    Report,* October 7, 1996.

## ELECTRONIC MEDIA

Internet web sites of the National Aeronautics and Space
Administration, including: www.nasa.gov (NASA news and
general information), www.jsc.nasa.gov (Johnson Space
Center, including astronaut biographies), www.hq.nasa.gov
(NASA headquarters, including historical information), and
www.station.nasa.gov (International Space Station details).

## PHOTO   ACKNOWLEDGMENTS

Photographs are reproduced by permission of the National Aeronautics and Space Administration, pp. 2, 6, 9, 11, 14, 16, 18, 27,
33 (all), 43, 46, 52, 57, 60, 64, 65, 68, 72, 73, 76, 80, 83, 87, 90, 94,
98, 106; the Smithsonian Institution, p. 23 (number 90-6836); Sov-
foto/Eastfoto, pp. 34, 38, 49, 51; and the U.S. Space and Rocket
Center®, p. 102.

Front and back cover images are reproduced courtesy of the
National Aeronautics and Space Administration.

# INDEX

# ABOUT THE AUTHOR

Carole S. Briggs has published many books for young people. She is an aviation enthusiast who loves to write about flight and space exploration. Briggs lives with her husband and two sons in Madison, Wisconsin.